"The Nonprofit Board Therapist offers much wise advice that can we can all benefit from."

Risa Lavizzo-Mourey, M.D., M.B.A.
President and CEO
Robert Wood Johnson Foundation

"The Nonprofit Board Therapist is a must read for any nonprofit board member and especially board leadership, the case studies and real life examples tackle the most challenging aspects of serving on a nonprofit board. Dennis not only points out the important issues, he offers realistic, step-by-step suggestions on how to deal with them.

Rob Brown- Board Chairman
Embrace Kids Foundation

"This book is a perfect guide for both CEO's and Board Members on the structure and strategies for creating a successful non-profit. Miller's practical, no nonsense approach is refreshing and will produce sustainable results."

Amy B. Mansue
President & CEO
Children's Specialized Hospital

"I sincerely value and respect Dennis Miller's practical straight forward approach. He always speaks to the heart of the matter with great wisdom and compassion. Dennis has a unique ability to assess a situation and clearly communicate years of experience in a concise and applicable forum. He is an inspiring and passionate man driven to helping others advance and achieve new levels of success."

Bill Tawpash
Executive Director, Metro New York
Children's Miracle Network

I was fortunate to have the opportunity to work directly with Dennis, implementing his recommendations for our board. The fundamentals outlined in this book will help build a broad base structure for any successful non- profit. These are sound, tried and true principles.

Thomas J McEvoy
Board Vice Chair
Make A Wish Foundation of NJ

"Dennis truly hits it out of the park in The Nonprofit Board Therapist. His ideas on board governance and engagement, that Development is NOT a department and his Investment vs. Tin Cup Theory are powerful messages for success!"

Barry Kirschner
Executive Director
The Valerie Fund

THE NONPROFIT BOARD THERAPIST: A GUIDE TO UNLOCKING YOUR ORGANIZATION'S TRUE POTENTIAL

Dennis C. Miller

authorHOUSE®

AuthorHouse™
1663 Liberty Drive
Bloomington, IN 47403
www.authorhouse.com
Phone: 1-800-839-8640

First published by AuthorHouse 6/14/2010

ISBN: 978-1-4520-1841-6 (e)
ISBN: 978-1-4520-1840-9 (sc)

Printed in the United States of America
Bloomington, Indiana

This book is printed on acid-free paper.

To my wife Gladys
who has always encouraged me to
achieve my goals and pursue my dreams.

Her love and support
has allowed me to unlock my true leadership potential.

Contents

ACKNOWLEDGEMENTS

I wish to acknowledge and thank all of my friends and clients who have inspired me to write this book, especially John Mans, Tom Weatherall, Dr. Jerry Ryan and David Flood.

I especially wish to acknowledge and thank my wife, Gladys, for her support and inspiration for the past 30 years, along with the love of my two sons, David and Douglas, and our dog, Bailey.

I also want to thank Wendy Dodge for all of her tireless work as my editor. I am forever grateful and appreciative of her love for the English language and efforts to make me look good. Finally, I want to thank Tom DePrenda for doing a great job designing the book's front and back covers.

INTRODUCTION

Over the past thirty years, I've had the unique opportunity to wear "many hats." I was the president and chief executive officer of a major nonprofit organization, the president of a successful healthcare foundation, and the chairman of the board of a private college preparatory school. I served as chairman of a capital campaign and worked as a corporate executive of a publicly traded company that assisted nonprofit sector clients. Now I am an author and the president/founder of a company dedicated to helping the nonprofit sector in their pursuit of their goals – and of excellence.

Everyone faces enormous challenges within the nonprofit sector. This is true whether your mission is related to education, healthcare, human services, environment or arts/culture. All of you have great causes and purposeful missions that are being advanced through the efforts of dedicated professionals, board members and volunteers who believe in your organization. Everyone has great hopes and dreams for his or her organization and is very proud to be associated with it! However, many still struggle to reach the level of excellence their mission requires. They struggle to fully engage their boards and key stakeholders and/or develop the resources needed to survive, let alone succeed or excel.

As a chief executive, you may ask, "How do I engage and motivate my board to be truly passionate about our mission and actively participate with confidence in our philanthropic initiatives?" As a board member, you may seek to learn, "How do I contribute to engaging my community in fully supporting our mission?" Or, as the board chair, you may want to know, "How do I recruit and develop board members who can assist me in achieving the dreams and goals of our nonprofit organization?"

In my first book, "A Guide to Achieving New Heights: The Four Pillars of Successful Nonprofit Leadership," my goal was to provide an inspirational and educational book on "how to unlock" the leadership potential of individuals (including chief executives, board members and those who aspire to leadership positions) in the nonprofit sector. In this book, I want to share my experience wearing many hats - and working with many nonprofit groups - to develop an organizational culture that inherently thrives on creating success.

As you read this book, you will learn from my experiences, observations of many colleagues, and the success achieved by my clients on how to *unlock your organization's true potential*. Though I have observed the success of many organizations, I have also seen too many organizations that never achieve the level of success they desire because they fail to fully understand the importance of integrating all key organization components. Those that fail to meet aggressive fundraising goals often wonder, despite their critical mission, why they did not raise "enough" money. Too often, they failed to see that they never fully integrated their governance, leadership, visioning and philanthropy efforts.

In the United States, there are approximately 1.3 million nonprofit organizations serving a wide range of important missions: arts/cultural, education, environmental, healthcare, human services, and other important areas. Many organizations have achieved national recognition and many thousands of nonprofits have demonstrated outstanding performance throughout their local communities. Yet, despite the tremendous sweat and tears that people poured into their nonprofit organization, far too many have failed to achieve their goals or operate at their full potential. In tough times, too many nonprofit organizations that provide critical services must unduly limit their services, or close their doors for lack of resources.

I have seen numerous highly successful organizations develop their potential by constantly improving who they are, what they do, and how they communicate their success and achievements. These organizations all exhibit one important characteristic, the deep commitment to excellence in all facets of their organizational life. They integrate strong board governance, leadership development, visioning, and philanthropy. They have the courage to constantly re-examine their board and leadership performance to make any necessary improvements, despite how uncomfortable those changes may seem at first. They are led by confident and competent chief executives and board leaders who inspire everyone in the organization to seek new ways to achieve their goals.

My goal in "The Nonprofit Board Therapist" is to provide a road map on how to unlock the true potential of your nonprofit organization. I hope that this book will inspire and motivate you to find the courage and develop the confidence to pursue your organization's dreams and goals. This book includes the following chapters:

+ Improving Board Governance
+ Increasing Leadership Potential
+ Releasing the Power of Visioning
+ Untapping Philanthropic Success
+ Bringing it All Together

The truth is that *unlocking your organization's true potential* is very rewarding, but it does not come about easy. Those organizations that have achieved this level of success have worked for years to create the right culture. With insight from this book, strong determination, and a commitment to making the necessary changes, your organization can overcome some of the common obstacles and achieve similar success. I have also included in each chapter a series of questions for you to answer that may help you *unlock your organization's true potential*. Whether your organization's obstacles are poor board governance, ineffective leadership, a stale vision that no longer motivates or inspires your stakeholders, and/or a lackluster fundraising strategy, if you follow the key steps outlined in this book, you will be on your way to a very exciting journey to strengthen your organization.

Each chapter will include an actual case story that demonstrates how the organization worked to *unlock their true potential*.

You will come away from reading this book with:

1. A road map to understanding and dramatically improving your organization's culture of success.

2. The determination to evaluate your organization against the best practices described in the book.

3. The hope, courage and motivation to achieve better results with your organization.

4. A sense of purpose that empowers and enables you to feel better about what you can do, thereby allowing you to approach your work with passion, high energy and a positive attitude.

You can help your organization *unlock its true potential* that will not only ensure its survival, but enable your organization to succeed for many years to come.

Although there may be a particular chapter in "The Nonprofit Board Therapist" that you may want to read first, you should read this book in its entirety. In this way, you will gain a better understanding of the role that integrating effective board governance, leadership development, visionary thinking and philanthropy play in the creation of a great nonprofit organization.

As you begin your journey through this book, consider these questions about your organization's readiness to journey with you:

+   Does your organization "stand above the herd" today?
+   Has your organization successfully competed for donors and dollars, despite today's economic difficulties?
+   Are all of your board members truly passionate about your mission and engaged in attaining its vision?

+ Does your board actively participate in philanthropic initiatives with confidence or with fear?
+ Do you know what great boards and great leaders do that make them different from their peers?
+ Have you learned to communicate your organization's achievements, results and measurements of success?

IMPROVING BOARD GOVERNANCE

"If you have built castles in the air, your work need not be lost: that is where they should be. Now put the foundations under them."
Henry David Thoreau

The roles and responsibilities of boards and their members have been well researched and written about by experts in the field. Based upon my experience, knowing what to do and actually doing it are two different things. To *unlock your organization's true potential*, boards need to constantly re-examine their own performance and make the necessary improvements that have been identified through their assessment process.

This chapter will address the following ways to improve your board's governance:

- ✦ Selecting the Board Chair
- ✦ Evaluating the Board's Structure, Committees and Meetings
- ✦ Reappointing Board Members
- ✦ Measuring the Level of Engagement and Motivation of the Board

This chapter will also help address the following questions:

- ✦ Why are some nonprofit organizations successful and others not?
- ✦ Why do some become good organizations and some become great?
- ✦ What are some of the differences between good boards and great boards?
- ✦ What are some of the common board obstacles to success and how do we effectively remove them?

SELECTING THE BOARD CHAIR

The chair (or president) of the board of directors plays an extremely important role in a nonprofit organization. The chair and the chief executive are the two key people in steering a nonprofit organization towards its vision. There needs to be a positive relationship between the chair of the board and the chief executive. A good chair works with the chief executive behind the scenes and stays in close communication with all members of the board. The chair of the board keeps track on the work of each board committee, plans meeting agendas, leads assessments of the board and chief executive, and helps recruit new board members.

As successfully outlined in "The Board Chair Handbook," written by William and Linda Dietel, the duties of the nonprofit board chair bear little resemblance to the job of a "for profit" board chair. Often in the "for profit" world, the chair of the board is also the chief executive officer, and thus involved in managing the organization's overall operation. This is not true for most nonprofits. The board chair focuses on the big picture, keeping an eye on the institution's mission, vision, and long term sustainability. As the leader of the board, the chair helps the board as a whole to think strategically about the organization's achievements for mission, vision and long-term goals, in the context in which it operates.

The board chair must be a strong strategic thinker who is able to make difficult decisions and willing to be accountable for the organization's sustainability. The role of the chair differs from organization to organization and even within an organization as it evolves over time. While the board chair is the chief volunteer officer and is charged with leading the board, the entire weight of the board's work does not fall completely on the shoulders of one person. Rather, because the board should speak with one voice, responsibility is shared by the board as a whole. The board chair needs to delegate to and empower board members, encouraging each of them to take ownership of their assigned responsibilities. Therefore, selecting the best person available for the board chair is crucial to *creating a culture of success.*

Here are ten specific actions that can be undertaken to identify and appoint your board chair:

1. *Immediately begin to assess the leadership talent of current board members.* Unless it is absolutely necessary, it is preferable to identify your new board chair from current members. It takes time to get to know your organization and the various issues that it is confronting. The role of the chair is better served by a current member.

2. *Ask your current board chair to begin as soon as possible to identify potential candidates.* The chair can begin a series of discussions with

the candidates regarding their interest in assuming the board chair role when the current chair's term expires. It is the responsibility of the board chair to develop a successor. The board chair should also begin to "nurture and develop" the successor the day that the board chair-elect is appointed.

3. *Institute ongoing board training for all board members* in all aspects of governance: bylaws, board structure and committees, strategic planning, fundraising, etc. There should be an annual retreat supplemented by other forms of educational programming for board members throughout the year.

4. *Offer the chair-elect a professional board coach/ mentor* to support the transition during the first year in office. Having a trusted professional available to "lend an ear" to the issues facing the new chair and offering practical solutions builds confidence. Just knowing that there is someone to turn to makes the job "less lonely" at the top.

5. *Ensure that the work of the board is done efficiently,* including: establishing the agenda, running meetings, communicating with other board members and receiving timely information from all committees. When the work of the board runs "smoothly," it is easier to recruit someone to assume the top spot!

6. *Find ways to reward and recognize your board members for the job they do.* Everyone likes to be recognized for their efforts, whether

volunteer or paid staff. Invite board members to socialize outside of the work place. Building relationships helps to motivate people to want to get further involved and provide the necessary leadership to further the mission. Remember, the old saying "all work and no play" doesn't help recruit a board chair.

7. *Provide opportunities for all board members to participate* in a wide array of committees, task forces and advisory boards to allow them to grow and demonstrate their leadership abilities. The more experience and knowledge board members have of the organization, the more comfortable they will feel when accepting the board leadership role.

8. *Highlight the organization and its "culture of success."* Organizations that continuously strive for excellence create a winning culture. Individuals are more likely to want to join a board and eventually lead an organization's board when it is perceived by everyone as a "winner" and "the place to be."

9. *Recognize former board chairs,* either through a formal recognition at an annual benefit event or through the creation of a "Chairpersons Club." Make the role of the board chair something special that is looked upon very favorably. This will surely make it more attractive for someone to seek and accept the important role.

10. *Recognize and address the reasons that appointing a board chair is difficult,* such as:

- Perception that the job requires too much time and too much work
- Too much board politics or bureaucracy
- A lack of "preparedness" or board training by the candidates
- The current board chair cannot relinquish control
- Board structures and committees are not properly set up and/or board roles are poorly defined, leaving the impression that the board chair has to do all the work
- Forgetting to consider leadership potential among board members

Recognizing some of the reasons that appointing a board chair is difficult can help you take early actions that will eliminate this difficulty. Nonprofit organizations that are able to successfully transition their board's leadership in an effective manner will benefit everyone that is served by the mission of the organization.

> *"The person who figures out how to harness*
> *the collective genius of his or her organization*
> *is going to blow away the competition."*
> Walter Wriston

EVALUATING THE BOARD'S STRUCTURE, COMMITTEES AND MEETINGS

The type of board and committee structure that is best for your organization can be determined by the current life cycle of your organization. In the well written book "Governance as Leadership: Reframing the Work of

Nonprofit Boards" written by Richard P. Chait, et al., the authors described the four stages of board governance: founding, fiduciary, strategic and leadership:

1. A founding board does almost all of the work, often without any paid staff. This is the primary role of a board in a new and developing organization.

2. A fiduciary role generally emerges after the staff has been hired to carry on the work. Here the board sets goals, policies and direction for the staff to implement.

3. As an organization matures, the board takes on a more strategic role and works together with the staff to develop and implement the strategic plan.

4. The fourth stage of a board's developing role is one of leadership. Though both the fiduciary and strategic roles remain important, providing leadership to the organization "in partnership" with the chief executive is the ideal role for an organization desiring to *create a culture of success*. In this stage, board governance is accomplished by asking the right questions, putting forth new ideas and challenges, and partnering with the chief executive to continually refresh and renew the organization's goals.

I encourage you to consider:

+ What stage of board governance does your organization need?
+ Is the majority of time at your board meetings spent on reporting the past or discussing the future?
+ Have your founding board members been able to let go of control or do they remain very involved in daily operations?
+ Does your chief executive nurture the leadership potential of those on the board?
+ Does your board evaluate each committee's purpose and goals on an annual basis?
+ Does your executive committee create the perception of "an inner and outer board?"

Based on my experience, the best board structure is one that is kept as simple as possible. Although vision is discussed in a later chapter, my recommendation is to develop your organization's vision before designing the needed board structure.

Committees are developed to help the board do the work that is required. The fewer the standing committees, the better. Each committee needs a chair that is appointed by the board chair. Goals for each committee need to be established that reflect the overall goals of the organization. Each committee should be evaluated annually to determine if it is achieving its goals, contributing to the overall success of the board, is appropriately sized and populated. It is highly desirable to have board and non-board members on each committee. Appointing non-board members to committees creates an excellent "farm system" for new board members. Committees should not meet just to meet. If there are no important action items on your board or committee agenda, consider canceling the meeting. *Unlocking your organization's true potential* requires board members who are highly motivated and engaged. Having them attend unnecessary meetings accomplishes the exact opposite.

> *"Once an organization loses its spirit of pioneering and rests on its early work, its progress stops."*
> *Thomas J. Watson, Sr.*

I believe that there are two committees which require further discussion – the executive committee and governance committee.

Executive Committee: The purpose of the executive committee should be to meet during an emergency when it would be difficult to convene the full board to meet. This is often the case when a board resolution must be approved for banking issues or grant funding applications. The executive committee is the only committee that has the power and authority to make decisions for the board. The executive committee can also be a "sounding board" for the chief executive who wishes to discuss key issues prior to presenting them to the full board. However, too often executive committees are scheduled inappropriately, creating the impression that there is "an inner board and an outer board, " especially to those not on the executive committee. Your board may want to consider having the executive committee meetings during the months when the full board is not meeting.

Governance Committee: The governance committee, in my opinion, is the most important committee of the board. Traditionally, nonprofit boards had nominating committees to recruit and recommend new board members. The term nominating committee implies a primary responsibility for recruiting new members. Over time, boards also realized that educating new and current members on a wide array of topics was also important throughout the terms of the members. Discovering that everyone benefits from education, not just new members, this committee's name evolved into the "board development committee." However, that name often became confused with the development committee charged with fundraising. Thus, the newly adopted term for board recruitment and development is the governance committee.

The governance committee has the following key responsibilities:

1. Periodically review and update the roles and responsibilities of the board (as a whole) as well as individual board members.
2. Assess the current and future board composition requirements and develop a profile of the board as it should evolve over time.
3. Identify potential new board members.
4. Nominate new individuals and reappoint current members.
5. Assess board effectiveness on an annual basis.
6. Periodically review and update board practices and policies.

7. Ensure board and chief executive succession planning.
8. Nominate board members for election as board officers.
9. Plan and schedule board retreats.
10. Provide ongoing education to all board members on important governance issues.

Other key committees of the Board often include finance, audit, human resources and compensation, strategic planning, development and investments. Effective board meetings require prior planning with the board chair and chief executive. They should discuss the key action items that will be required for approval, any anticipated obstacles, and the amount of time being allotted for each item when preparing the meeting agenda. It is very important for the board chair to keep the meeting moving and preventing "too much stray" of the agenda. No one wants to attend unproductive meetings that run on unnecessarily.

> *"The achievements of an organization are the results of the combined efforts of each individual."*
> *Vince Lombardi*

I would also like to mention briefly the appropriate use of advisory boards and task forces. Advisory boards can be a very effective tool when utilized appropriately and when misused can be a public relations disaster. Many organizations create advisory boards to solicit advice on a specific issue and wish to gather individuals from the community who may have the expertise needed. The key to success with advisory boards is simple: make sure that the members understand their purpose, give them specific responsibilities and listen to their advice. If you are going to ask someone for their "advice," make sure you "act" upon it when given. Too many advisory boards are created to "find a place" for older board members or because it looks like a great idea at the time. The enthusiasm of those invited to serve on the advisory board often dissipates quickly and the gap between expectation and performance is enormous.

A task force is different from an advisory board in that it is established for a specific objective, such as planning a retreat or to review by-laws, within a specific period of time. Upon completion of the work, the group disbands.

REAPPOINTING BOARD MEMBERS

One of the major responsibilities of the governance committee is to ensure that a process is in place to evaluate an individual board member's performance prior to rewarding that member with a new term. In order to *unlock your organization's true potential*, the board must continually evaluate each member's performance and make the difficult decision to not reappoint when it is appropriate and in the best interest of the board. This process really begins during the recruitment and orientation process, by explaining the expectations of each new member. It continues during each year through the board's educational activities and annual goal setting procedures. The expectations of each board member and the board as a whole should be an ongoing conversation. It should never be a surprise when a decision is made by the governance committee not to reappoint someone to the board.

If your board does not have a reappointment process, which includes a fact-based evaluation of individual performance against expectations, it should be developed. Key aspects of this process are:

- Preparing a written job description for board members
- Keeping attendance records for board and committee meetings
- Developing a target profile for representation (e.g., functions, professions, diversity, etc.) that you want for the board
- Creating an annual checklist to evaluate the contributions of board members whose terms will expire

One final issue that I feel is very important to discuss is knowing when and how to fire a board member. Everyone knows that board members are a tremendous asset, providing needed expertise and leadership in furthering the mission and success of an organization. However, occasionally an individual board member is not contributing or worse, can become destructive to the organization. The destructive or "disruptive" behavior can become a negative force to the workings of the board and executive team, resulting in poor morale among board and staff, loss of energy, increased board turnover and/or a damaged public opinion.

The following are examples of "disruptive" behavior:

- Ongoing poor preparation, participation and lack of attendance at board meetings
- A lack of understanding of the board member's role
- Failing to become a team player by accepting the consensus of the board after issues are fully debated and voted upon

- ✦ Consistently failing to follow through on tasks and responsibilities
- ✦ Not making a personal contribution as a board member
- ✦ Undermining the board or board officer or chief executive
- ✦ Not maintaining confidentiality on board matters
- ✦ Consistently failing to live up to the values promoted by the organization

> *"You can tell more about a person by*
> *what they say about others than you can*
> *by what others say about him."*
> *Anonymous*

When these behaviors are exhibited, the board chair (not the chief executive) has the responsibility to meet with the board member and discuss the behavior and the impact it is having on the organization. Often, the board member will become aware of the behavior and make the necessary changes. However, when the discussion or counseling fails to solve the problem, the board member may need to be asked to resign. If the board doesn't face up to its responsibility, the problem could become a disaster for the organization and have long-term negative effects. Just as the board holds the chief executive accountable and responsible for behavior, the board must do the same for its members.

How does one go about "firing" a board member? This is easier said than done. Boards are made up of people and no one enjoys having to deal with confrontation, especially with regard to a professional colleague. The following are three suggestions for dealing with this situation:

1. *Have the board chair and another member of the governance committee or executive committee meet with the disruptive board member.* This discussion should strongly inform the board member about the negative implications of the behavior in question and the possibility of requesting the person's removal from the board.

2. *Monitor ongoing behaviors.* If the disruptive behavior does not change, the chair should contact members of the governance committee to discuss removing the member from the board. If the governance committee recommends the person's removal, a special meeting of the board should be called (without the person in question attending) and a vote taken to remove the member. Your board may want to ask legal counsel to review the situation to ensure that the board's actions comply with the organization's bylaws.

3. *Consider having the governance committee review the situation surrounding this member and consider not recommending a renewed term.* The committee's recommendation for non-renewal should also go to the executive committee for a vote, if that is deemed necessary.

It is highly suggested that the board chair inform the individual member involved of the board's decision and allow the board member to resign and save face.

The removal of an individual from the board can be a humiliating experience and there is no need to make this a personal indictment. One should apply the Golden Rule in this situation; always treat the person the way that you would want to be treated in this situation. One positive outcome of the experience of having to remove a board member should be a more thorough review of the board's recruitment, reappointment and orientation programs. Implementation of performance assessments (for both the board and individual board members) is helpful on an annual basis.

While the vast majority of board members volunteer their time, energy and talent to their organizations, we must remember that they also accept the responsibility and accountability that comes with agreeing to serve on the board. To *unlock your organization's true potential*, every board member needs to work together towards achieving the goals of the organization, bringing fulfillment and meaning to all who serve in such a wonderful role.

MEASURING THE LEVEL OF ENGAGEMENT AND MOTIVATION OF THE BOARD

One of the more overlooked responsibilities of a nonprofit board is the requirement to assess its own performance. Nonprofit boards are generally familiar with their main responsibilities, such as selecting the chief executive, evaluating the chief executive's performance, recruiting new members, developing succession plans, and ensuring that the organization has the necessary resources to carry out its mission. However, they often forget to evaluate how well those responsibilities are being executed, or how they feel about their role as a member of the board.

There are two credible options for the board to assess its own performance:

1. Complete a board assessment questionnaire that asks a series of questions on the work of the board with a scaled response, such as 1 (lowest/strongly disagree) to 5 (highest/strongly agree).

2. Have a professional facilitator perform the assessment with a combination of a questionnaire and confidential interviews, including open-ended questions. These questions can help measure the board member's engagement with the organization, how fulfilling and meaningful their experience as a board member has been, and what, if any, recommendations they have to remove obstacles and improve the work of the board.

> *"Look within, for within is the wellspring*
> *of virtue, which will not cease flowing,*
> *if you cease not from digging."*
> Marcus Aurelius

The vast majority of boards that perform an annual assessment utilize a questionnaire format. Questions call for a numerical response on a wide range of issues dealing with the organization's mission, programs and services, financial resources, fiscal oversight, CEO performance, board and CEO relationships, new board member orientation, meetings and other board policies. A summary is usually prepared after all of the responses have been obtained. The relative numerical score indicates areas of strength as well as potential areas for improvement. The advantage to this approach is the ease of execution and timeliness of the reports. On the other hand, the problem with most, if not all, questionnaires is that they don't easily allow for open ended questions that get to "the heart of the matter" for improving the work of the board. Questionnaires are better than nothing, but may be insufficient for a thorough assessment.

> *"Albrecht's Law – Intelligent people,*
> *when assembled into an organization,*
> *will tend toward collective stupidity."*
> *Karl Albrecht*

From my experience, the most effective way to assess the nonprofit board's performance is to combine a questionnaire with a trained board facilitator who can ask important open-ended questions that will also measure the level of engagement and motivation of the board members. This approach can be done periodically, to augment an annual questionnaire. Some key questions that need to be asked include:

- How would you describe the board's passion for the mission of the organization?
- How passionate are you about the mission?
- What is the "vision" for this organization?
- How do you feel about the organization's current strategic plan?
- What recommendations, if any, would you make to improve the process and the plan?

- How would you describe your level of excitement about seeing this vision become a reality?
- What do you like about being on this board?
- How meaningful and fulfilling has your experience been serving on this board? Why?
- How would you describe your level of engagement with this organization? Why?
- How would you describe the board's level of engagement?
- How effective are the board meetings? What would make them better?
- What are the current strengths of the board?
- What areas of improvement are needed?
- What is the image of this organization in the community?
- What recommendations, if any, do you have for improving the image?
- How does the board measure the success of this organization?
- How does the board ensure that the organization provides value to its key stakeholders?
- How would you describe the strengths of the chief executive?
- How would you describe the chief executive's communication style?
- What recommendations, if any, would you make to improve the chief executive's performance?
- Who should succeed the chief executive should the position suddenly become vacant?

+ How would you describe the board's relationship with the chief executive?
+ What is the board's role in fundraising?
+ What recommendations, if any, would you make to improve the board's role in fundraising?
+ Do you make an annual personal gift to the organization?

To dramatically improve the work of the board, one has to assess the level of engagement and motivation of their board members. Only through engaging and motivating all members on their boards can nonprofits truly *unlock their organization's true potential.*

Questions:
+ Has your board performed a comprehensive assessment of its own performance recently?
+ Could your organization benefit from such a performance assessment today?

Let's now turn to increasing your leadership potential.

CASE STUDY
IMPROVING BOARD GOVERNANCE

Make-A-Wish Foundation of New Jersey

Thomas P. Weatherall is one of the most passionate and inspirational leaders I have had the pleasure to meet. As President and CEO of one of the largest and more efficient Chapters of Make-A-Wish Foundation, Tom has provided the leadership, inspiration and passion to ensure that every child with a life-threatening medical condition in New Jersey has the ability to have his or her "wish" come true. Make-A-Wish Foundation of New Jersey has granted more than 7,500 wishes to children since its inception in 1983 to enrich the human experience with hope, strength and joy. In order to fund the granting of these wishes, the Chapter raises $6 million a year, ranking them in the top five Chapters nationally. While other CEOs may be happy with this level of success, Tom's passion drives him to constantly seek new levels of success, knowing there are always more children who have a "wish" to be granted.

Tom and his board chair knew that to achieve this higher level of success, they needed to further engage their board members in the strategic and philanthropic initiatives of the Chapter. Tom contacted our firm, Dennis C. Miller Associates, Inc., to perform a comprehensive board performance assessment to identify ways to further engage and motivate the board.

We commenced our performance assessment of the board in two ways. First, we requested a list of informational items to review including board plans, actions and discussions related to vision and goal setting, board minutes for the past year, strategic plans, board recruitment plans, current board committee structure and purpose, by-laws and board leadership succession planning. Second, we confidentially interviewed all board members as well as the Chapter's executive team. Conducting board interviews are an extremely important tool in assessing the board's performance. Utilizing questionnaires alone rarely results in dramatic improvement in the board's work. They fail to measure the level of the board's passion, engagement and connection to the organization.

A report of our findings and recommendations was presented to the Board of Directors. Our report highlighted the strengths of the board while offering a list of recommendations for improving the work of the board and increasing their level of engagement. One of the more important recommendations dealt with the Chapter's use of their executive committee. Too many board members felt that there was an "inner and outer" board. In order to fully engage the board, we recommended that this committee meet only when an emergency issue must be dealt with and then to make sure all actions are reported back to the full board at the next board meeting. Another important recommendation was to create a governance committee to replace the current board nominating committee. In addition to board recruitment, there was no formal process in place to reappoint current board members. Finally, a series of detailed recommendations was made to more effectively use the talents and skills of the board members on other board committees as well as the appropriate use of advisory and honorary boards.

The Chapter's board unanimously approved the report's full list of recommendations, developed a priority list of those that needed to be completed first, and appointed a steering committee to ensure the successful implementation of all recommendations. Based on follow up meetings with Tom and the Board leadership team, the Chapter is on track to reach the next level of success and grant more wishes. Tom would have not settled for anything less. I am proud to call him my friend as well as my client.

INCREASING LEADERSHIP POTENTIAL

"Each time someone stands up for an ideal, or acts to improve the lot of others, or strikes out against an injustice, he sends forth a tiny ripple of hope."
Robert F. Kennedy

Similar to those of the board, the roles and responsibilities of the chief executive have also been well described in numerous books and research articles. Other than the board chair, the chief executive is the most important person in the organization with responsibilities for carrying out the mission and achieving the vision of the organization. Why do some chief executives exhibit remarkable leadership while others simply become good managers at best but never develop the leadership potential necessary to successfully guide their organizations to *unlock the organization's true potential?*

This chapter will address ways to increase your leadership potential by discussing the following:

- ✦ Passion and Inspiration
- ✦ Building Relationships
- ✦ Establishing Trust and Respect
- ✦ Making People Feel Good about Themselves
- ✦ Listening to your Team

+ Establishing your Credibility
+ Delivering on your Promises
+ Managing by "Being Seen"
+ Being a Decision Maker
+ Being Fair and Flexible
+ Networking – Developing External Relationships
+ Mentoring and Coaching
+ Being Business Minded
+ Succession Planning and Leadership Transition
+ Creating the Vision

"Leadership is the art of getting someone else to do something you want done because he wants to do it."
Dwight D. Eisenhower

Leadership has been defined as the art of motivating a group of people to act towards achieving a common goal. The most important characteristic of a leader is the decision to become a leader. At some point in time, a person decides that they want to provide others with a vision, direct the course of future events and inspire others to succeed. One major question that is always asked is the "nature versus nurture" question - are people born leaders or do they choose to become leaders? Volumes of research have been written on the subject and an in-depth discussion is beyond the scope of this book. However, Daniel Maltby, Ph.D., wrote in "The State of Leadership Theory and Training – Leaders: Born or Made" that the current consensus is that it is both. Genetics and early family experiences play the significant role in developing the personality and character needs that motivate the individual to lead. They also contribute to the development of the intellectual and interpersonal skills necessary to lead.

According to Maltby, the majority of researchers today believe that the origins of leadership go beyond genes and family to other sources. Work experiences, hardship, opportunity, education, role models and mentors all go together to craft a leader. An important assumption in this theory is that the raw material essential in people in order to lead is not scarce. The lack of needed leaders is a reflection of neglected development, rather than a dearth of abilities. There seems to be no substitute for learning through doing, making mistakes and improving with time.

I strongly believe that individuals can dramatically increase their leadership potential by seeking opportunities for personal growth, building self esteem, increasing self awareness and seeking feedback from their colleagues and mentors. However, the best designed programs of leadership development are contingent on the motivation of the candidate.

Passion and Inspiration

> *"A small body of determined spirits fired*
> *by an unquenchable faith in their mission*
> *can alter the course of history."*
> *Mohandas Gandhi*

Being passionate about your organization and its vision and mission is crucial to your success. Passion is a strong, powerful emotion, enthusiasm, fondness or desire for anything. In order to increase your leadership potential, you need to demonstrate and exhibit your passion. People in your organization will become inspired by you since passion is contagious. Passion generates a great deal of positive excitement and willingness on everyone's part to contribute to the organization's success. Increasing your effective use of the power of emotions will help you to unleash your leadership potential.

Questions:
+ How passionate and inspirational are you?
+ Is your organization's leadership inspiring others?
+ What can you do to further demonstrate your passion?

Building Relationships

What is it that makes a winning organization so effective? In winning organizations, people make the difference. It's not the buildings and equipment, nor the hardwood floor on the stage, or the equipment in the operating room. It's the people - the internal people who provide the services and the external people who affect and are affected by the organization - who make the organization a winner. In order to increase one's leadership potential, an effective leader must know how to build strong relationships with people.

Building strong relationships is the key to success. This belief is often viewed as soft, emotional, and irrelevant to an organization's success. However, those organizations whose leaders are able to bring out the best in others, whose leaders are able to make people feel important, whose leaders make people feel that their voices, concerns and actions do matter, those are the organizations that will be successful.

Questions:
+ What are the most effective organizations you know?
+ How would you describe the relationship the leaders of those organizations have with their stakeholders?
+ How would members of your team describe the relationship the CEO has with them?

> *"The pessimist complains about the wind. The optimist expects it to change. The leader adjusts the sails."*
> *John Maxwell*

Establishing Trust and Respect

The organizations whose leaders have the trust of their employees, whose leaders are respected and have credibility, perform better than organizations whose leaders lack these qualities. As in any team sport, goals are achieved on a team basis; you cannot do it alone. No man is an island. Smart leaders realize that to be successful, they must get the most out of people. You get the most out of people when you are trusted, respected and viewed as credible.

You may have formal authority through your formal status in your organization and your job description. However, people's respect is really gained through your informal authority: people's trust and admiration for you. You win hearts by your sincerity, passion, and vision.

Leaders who win hearts let employees know that they are there for the employees. This builds strong relationships.

For example, if you have trust in a marriage, the relationship is strengthened. It is the same in a workplace; if you build trust, the organization will be strengthened.

Questions:
+ How have you earned the trust of your employees?
+ What have you done to earn their respect?

To foster trust, talk to people at all levels. Tell them about your organization's plan and how they can participate in its success. Also, watch your actions because people will watch how you treat others and how you communicate with them.

Nonprofit organizations are in a very difficult and competitive environment. It requires a lot of skill, people, and hard work to accomplish your goals. A good leader is listened to, trusted, and respected. A good leader realizes that everyone contributes to an organization's success. If you are trusted and respected, they will work towards your organization's success.

Making People Feel Good about Themselves

As an old saying goes, people may not remember what you said, they may not remember what you did, but they will remember how you made them feel. From my experience running a major medical center, all people, whether head nurse or housekeeper, had a role to play in the medical center's success. My aim was to make them realize that the role they played in the medical center and their input were both important because productivity and accomplishing objectives is all based on getting people to realize that their individual goals are tied into the organization's goals.

Listening to your Team

How do you feel when you know that the person you're talking to is listening to you? You feel great, don't you? People want to be listened to. And as an effective leader, you need to listen to them. By listening to your people, you can stay abreast of everything that is happening in your organization. As a result, you know what issues you face. When you listen to people, you obtain valuable information which you may decide to act upon.

People want to be both listened to and heard. You must hear what is being said to understand how people think and feel. This enables you to get the most out of them.

> *"Coaches who can outline plays on a black board are a dime a dozen. The ones who win get inside their player and motivate."*
> *Vince Lombardi*

When I first became president of a medical center, I held meetings with employees at all levels called "Dialogue with the President" meetings. At these meetings, I let people know my management philosophy that patient satisfaction and employee satisfaction go hand in hand. After asking questions, I learned that to improve patient satisfaction, we had to improve employee satisfaction. By listening to people's concerns, you remove obstacles to your organization's success.

Hold periodic meetings with employees of all levels. State your vision and philosophy at these meetings. Also, don't just talk; hear their concerns, too.

Asking questions makes people feel that you listen to them, which makes them feel that you care. And if they feel that you care, they will be more productive.

When listening to people, you want to empower them. You do this by allowing them to come up with their own answers and solutions. Your aim is to simply provide them with the questions and the goals.

Establishing your Credibility

This is a key part of building relationships. You establish credibility by making decisions that benefit the organization, decisions that align with the organization's mission. When you consistently do this, you earn the people's trust and you earn their respect.

If you are new to your organization, or if you are trying to create a new environment that will enable you to reach new heights, there are things that you can do to immediately build credibility. For example, let people know the organization's values and what behavior is expected. Also, let them know that there are rules and regulations and that you expect them to be followed – by people at all levels. This lets people know that there is someone in charge. Set the example; people will watch both what you say and what you do.

People are looking for authority; they want to know that there is someone in charge. When employees sense that something is wrong which needs to be corrected (such as another employee's performance or some safety issue) and they know that someone is addressing the situation, they feel better. That's where your credibility gets built. Also, to establish credibility (and, therefore, build strong relationships), you must be able to make decisions, too. (I'll discuss this in more depth later.)

Delivering on your Promises

It is imperative that you keep your promises. However, if you've made a commitment that you can no longer keep, own up to it. Let people know the reasons why your position has changed. They make not like your decision, however, telling them your reasons for the change lets them know that you have integrity. If you make a promise to do something, deliver on it and if you cannot, be up front about it.

> *"Losers make promises they often break. Winners make commitments they always keep."*
> Denis Waitley

Managing by "Being Seen"

When was the last time you got out from behind your desk and walked around? Too often, I've heard people say, "I never see the boss." Effective leaders manage by walking around. When people say, "I never see the boss," this decreases trust and weakens the relationship. Yes, I understand that you have a lot of external responsibilities, but it goes back to employees feeling connected to you. If they see you, they will feel connected to you and you will get the best from them.

When things are difficult in the organization, it is even more important that you walk around. Don't be panicky; this will create panic in everybody else. Instead, when you walk around, let people see that you are calm and that you are in charge. Being an employee-focused leader who is seen comes back to you ten times over.

Why have presidents of the United States visited cities? They wanted to be seen and to get their messages out. Let people see who you are. Stop by and say "hi" to the person in the back office. You cannot imagine how important this is to your organization. Let them know you are just there to see how things are going. Sometimes people will be intimidated. Others may think that you are there because something is wrong. Commit to "being seen" with your employees as part of your regular week work practice. Spend a certain amount of time getting out there introducing yourself and it will come back to you many times over.

Being a Decision Maker

When I first became president of the medical center, there was a cultural change program already under way to improve "customer satisfaction and employee empowerment." However, the way this was being implemented by the outside consultants actually had the opposite effect of demoralizing the staff. One of the first things I did was eliminate the program. Nurses cheered.

People need to know that there is a leader, that someone is steering the ship. They need to know that when a tough decision has to be made that there is someone up there who will make the decision. When you're on a plane, you want to know that there is someone on board who is in charge. Your employees feel the same way in your organization.

Let people know, through your actions, that you are the leader, that you are going to make the tough decisions and that you will take on the challenges through a core set of values that you work with. This doesn't mean that you make everyone comfortable; sometimes you will need to issue challenges and shake things up. Sometimes you will ask tough questions and sometimes people will feel uncomfortable. However, you do these things with a core set of values.

> *"Tell me and I forget; show me and I*
> *remember; involve me and I understand."*
> Anonymous

Successful leaders have a core set of values that they live and work by. These values are on display for all to see. You must have a core set of values and be an example of them because people are watching you. By having these core set of values and living them, you will be in a better position to achieve new heights. Winning organizations have leaders who live by the core values of the organization. Being a leader is really about demonstrating your values.

Have you ever worked for a person who just couldn't make a decision? Do you remember how frustrating that was? Effective leaders know how to make decisions. There is nothing better than having a leader who can make decisions in an appropriate and timely manner. It is a blessing to an organization.

Questions:
+ Are you avoiding making a tough decision?
+ If you are avoiding a tough decision, how is this affecting your organization?

In my first year as a medical center CEO, the most difficult thing I had to do was to terminate an employee. I was the first CEO in the medical center's history (as far as I know) to fire someone.

Firing someone is tough; however, effective leaders know that sometimes it must be done. Why? Employees know who is not performing. They know who isn't carrying out the organization's values. And since they know, they expect the leader to deal with it regardless of how difficult it is.

If you're the leader, you are expected to evaluate and terminate the non-performers because they have an impact on others. Yes, it is important to recognize people's contributions and to thank them and build trust. However, it is also your job to make sure that people who are not living up to your organization's values are terminated. It's often something that leaders avoid; they hope that the problem will go away – but it doesn't.

> *"I don't know the key to success, but the key to failure is trying to please everybody."*
> Bill Cosby

Being an effective leader is not a popularity contest. Sometimes you have to make the decision that is best for the 98% by removing the other 2%. When you remove the bad apples (and everyone knows who they are), you make room for new flowers to bloom.

Being Fair and Flexible

People are going to make mistakes, particularly if you empower them and try to develop them. Before you reprimand someone who has made a mistake, look at the consequences of a penalty you want to impose and ask if it is fair. Effective leaders know that to build strong relationships, sometimes you need to be compassionate and understanding. If a person has made a mistake, ask yourself if you would do better by giving the person a second chance. You must be as equitable and fair as possible – consistently.

Effective leaders understand where people are coming from and their intentions. Use your intuition and your gut. And most importantly, be flexible – don't just live by the book. Sure, people in the organization will make mistakes. However, sometimes people will climb higher and achieve more if they know that you are there for them. It's just like children playing on the monkey bars; they will climb higher and experience more when they know that someone they trust is there to catch them if they fall. I've given people breaks and helped them, and it has come back to me ten times over. I once found out that an employee was having problems in his personal life and confidentially arranged for him to get the professional support he and his family needed. Shortly therefore, he became one of our most productive employees.

Networking: Developing External Relationships

In addition to building relationships with your "internal family," it is equally important to develop strong relationships with all of your external constituents. As the leader of your organization, developing relationships with key community and business leaders, elected and appointed public officials and networking with fellow colleagues in your field is extremely important. Take the time and effort to get to know them the same way that you would members of your "internal family." Find out ways that you can help them. Ask them if there is anything that you can do for them and let them know that they can call you directly if they or someone they know needs the services of your organization. In order to be an effective leader, you must be viewed both "inside" and "outside" of your organization as a trusted and respected individual.

The main point of building relationships is that everyone is an important member of your organization. This includes your employees, management team, board members, volunteers, donors and external constituents. If you want to reach your goals and objectives and achieve your vision, you must inspire, empower, and motivate people. Let them know how well they are doing and where they need to improve. Pat them on the back when they do a good job. Go tell them that they've done a good job. It means a lot to them.

Also, give people a reward for a job well done. If they did a special job, give them a treat like a ticket to a ballgame or to a movie. You're going to achieve your objectives by working with others, so it makes sense to build your talent by getting the most out of your people. You do this by following the Golden Rule.

Mentoring and Coaching

Every successful person at some time in their life has had a mentor or friend who cared about them and took a personal interest in their personal career development. As a successful leader, seek opportunities to mentor others internal or external to your organization. Your experience and knowledge are vital to others in their professional development and what it takes to become a leader in their organization. Mentoring is a two-way mutually beneficial relationship where the mentor provides advice, shares knowledge and experiences to allow the individual to grow and develop at his or her own pace. This relationship is often informal and is a low pressure, self discovery type approach. Seeking mentoring opportunities is a great way to increase your leadership potential and gives you the satisfaction that comes from sharing and helping someone else.

Coaching is different than mentoring but is another great way to help others in your organization. Whereas mentoring usually has no agenda and is self selecting, coaching is performance related, has specific agendas and is often required for the person being coached to keep his or her job. A leader should coach those in their organization that need to develop certain skills for their responsibilities, challenges and performance expectations. The coach has an actual level of authority by nature of their position and can insist upon compliance. Whereas the mentoring relationship is reciprocal, the coaching relationship is more tutorial, observing someone's work and actions and provides advice on how to improve execution. Successful leaders want to help others in their personal and professional lives. By becoming a mentor or coach, you feel better about yourself for giving to others and thus, enhance your own leadership potential.

Being Business Minded

> *"Nobody ever lost money taking a profit."*
> *Bernard Baruch*

People who work in nonprofit organizations often think of themselves as not having to make a profit. It is almost as if they believe that stating that your organization is a nonprofit organization gives them a license to operate without a profit. However, the reality is that for your organization to further your mission and achieve your strategic vision, you must generate and maintain a positive operating margin. Whenever I worked for a nonprofit organization, I used to tell people that the organization is tax exempt, however, we must make a profit to survive.

Absolutely nothing sets an organization back more than constantly operating in the red. Your entire focus becomes centered on your negative operating margin. Maintaining current programs, developing new programs, investing in new facilities, etc., are all derailed when you cannot financially operate a positive bottom line.

Have you ever heard a business executive refer to someone as having a "nonprofit mentality?" Most of our colleagues who work for a tax exempt organization manage their organizations with a "nonprofit mentality." To lead your organization to achieve new heights, you must develop a new mindset, a new way of thinking about how your organization is managed financially. Stop thinking that your organization is a nonprofit. Instead, see it as being tax exempt. Whether you work for a theatre, shelter, school, or hospital, you must generate an operating margin to move your organization's mission forward. Remember, *nonprofit is your tax status, not your business plan.*

To achieve new heights, your organization must make a profit, and to make a profit, you must be business-minded. By "business-minded," I mean that you must run your nonprofit organization the same way you would run a profitable business. There are several things that you can do and focus on to be more business-minded.

*"It's easy to make a buck. It's a lot
tougher to make a difference."*
Tom Brokaw

Focus on both your mission *and* your margin. It is no longer sufficient to say, "Only my mission is important." I once worked for a large Catholic hospital that was very mission-oriented. I was recruited because of my strong operations and financial background. The President of the hospital, a Catholic nun who ruled with an iron fist, taught me the importance of mission along with the importance of patient care and taking responsibility for the care of those who could not afford to pay. Though I agreed with her in principle, my job was to remind the religious order that "without a margin, there will be no mission." We had to develop and implement sound business principles in our budgeting, revenue projections, expense management and account receivables. These sound business practices enabled our hospital to achieve a positive operating margin every year. These practices allowed us to maintain our mission for caring for the less fortunate in our community. Mission and margin go hand and hand. Without one, you cannot have the other.

Focus on revenue growth. You cannot cut your way to success; you must grow your way to success. With the growing demand for your services and the costs of labor, benefits, equipment, etc., you must grow your revenue. Grow your top line with aggressive fundraising, grants, new services, etc. Too many of us in the nonprofit world have hoped that money would flow from heaven and when it didn't, the board and staff went into crisis mode and focused on getting out of the operating deficit – often without a plan and the necessary skills.

Grow your way to success is the best motto to live by. If you ever talk to business owners whose businesses have failed, they will tell you that the main reason was lack of sales. Likewise, if you don't want your organization to fail, you want to focus on the top line. Grow your revenue; it is a lot easier to maintain your bottom line from the top.

One of the biggest differences that I have seen in the corporate world versus the nonprofit sector is the issue of holding people accountable for what they are responsible for. Usually in the nonprofit world, we assign responsibility without any accountability. However, it does no good to delegate if you do not hold people accountable. To provide the necessary leadership for your organization, you must develop a business mindset that holds people accountable for their actions. People need to know what is expected of them, what they are responsible for and that they are accountable for achieving the results required of them.

Too often I have seen what I call the "warm body" theory in managing nonprofit organizations which is to prefer to have any person with a beating heart to remain on the payroll regardless of their actual performance since "somebody is better than nobody." Develop your staff and give them the ingredients they need to grow. Give them as many of the tools they need as possible - and then hold them accountable for their work.

While it is important to hold people accountable, it is also extremely important to reward, recognize, and praise those whose performances are worthy of attention. It is good business to let employees know that you appreciate their efforts. I think the best way to do this is to verbally tell them. You could say something like, "Hey Joan, I just wanted to let you know that I heard what a great job you did last week organizing our new program and I greatly appreciate your efforts." How does this make Joan feel? It makes her feel terrific. Although it is also acceptable to write a personal note to her and to include a copy in her personnel file, expressing your appreciation in person is preferred.

"You can really change the world if you care enough."
Marion Wright Edelman

There are also many ways of rewarding your employees that have little to do with money. Sure, getting a generous raise is very rewarding, but we cannot always afford to do that. Though money is very important to all of us (we all need to pay the bills, mortgages, college tuition, etc.), positive feedback is the great motivator. I have found that the best time to give praise is close to the time when the employee actually earned it. Don't just wait for the annual performance review to tell someone that they did a good or bad job. Having a conversation with an employee about their annual performance should never be a surprise. Let them know what they are doing well and what they need to improve. Provide guidance and counseling when needed.

Questions:
+ How do you reward and recognize employees?
+ Do you feel comfortable publicly praising your staff?
+ Does your organization create incentives to achieve outstanding performance?

How many times have you seen a value statement of some organization (profit or nonprofit) that read something like this, "We value our employees and consider them our greatest asset." Yet, when asked how they develop and nurture their employees' potential, few nonprofit leaders can answer succinctly. As a leader of your organization, you need to develop a business practice that enables you to:

1. Hire the best people that you can.
2. Mentor as many as you can.
3. Delegate to others.
4. Allow others to grow, take risks and make mistakes.

Remember, whether your organization is a homeless shelter, theater group, children's cancer center, or school, it is a business and must be managed like one. Though you may not be responsible to corporate shareholders who financially invest in your company and who expect a good return for their investment, you are responsible to the community for preserving and continuing the mission, and that can only be achieved by obtaining a positive operating margin.

Succession Planning and Leadership Transition

According to a recognized national expert, succession planning is one of the most avoided conversations in the nonprofit community. Board members and CEOs are afraid to raise the issue for fear of sending the wrong signal or because they do not know what to do. In reality, succession planning is nothing more than developing a good insurance policy. It gives "peace of mind" and enhances the leadership skills among key staff. An effective and secure minded leader ensures that a succession plan is in place for his or her organization. Succession planning provides the know-how to sustain all operations and communicate with stakeholders in the event of the sudden departure of a CEO. It shouldn't wait until you are facing a potential crisis. It should begin now.

In addition, successful leaders create leadership plans for other key staff members and help "groom" their eventual replacement. Leadership transition planning is another sign of effective leadership. Developing positive leadership traits among skilled professionals on their staff boosts staff morale. A well done succession and leadership transition plan is also critical for the peace of mind of the board.

Creating the Vision

> *"The single defining quality of leaders is the*
> *capacity to create and realize a vision."*
> *William Bennis, On Becoming a Leader*

An effective and strong leader "visions" the future for the organization. Whereas mission answers the question, "Why do we exist?" vision answers the question "Where do we want to go?" This is an important question because a leader sets the course for a new direction or future view of the organization. It takes courage to set the vision. Leaders of nonprofits can get caught up in the day-to-day challenges of managing the organization. Still, a leader's responsibility is to create the vision and build a strategic plan to make that vision become a reality.

The old management theory was that the board set the vision and management implemented the plan to achieve it. Today, a leader must work in a true partnership with the board to create the future direction of the organization. Take the initiative in creating your organization's vision.

Effective leaders develop and communicate their vision first; they do not wait for their boards to create the vision.

Let's now turn to releasing the power of your organization's vision.

CASE STUDY
INCREASING LEADERSHIP POTENTIAL

Women's Breast Cancer Center

Holly, the Executive Director of the Women's Breast Cancer Center, and I met through a mutual friend at a professional league baseball game. The owner of the team is a very good friend of mine and introduced me to Holly, her then board chair and another key board member.

Holly, with the support from her board chair, requested my assistance as an executive mentor to improve her leadership ability. Holly felt that she was not getting the support she needed from her board and had recently received some negative comments during her performance review that were very upsetting to her. Holly wanted some outside help in resolving the issues she was having with some members of her board. I met privately with Holly to ascertain the issues that she wanted to resolve. Holly is very likeable and direct in her style of communication and I wanted to help her.

As part of my engagement, I met initially with each member of Holly's management team and all members of the Board of Directors. It was clear to me that the results achieved by Holly in fundraising and community relations were outstanding and I was confused by the negative comments from some of the board members. It was also clear to me that there was a great deal of confusion over the role of the board chair, the board members and their expectations of the Executive Director.

I met with the board chair and Holly and provided my observations and recommendations. I suggested that both of them could benefit from "coaching" and they agreed. A set of goals were established for both Holly, board chair and the board. Roles and responsibilities were provided for all of them. I proceeded to meet with Holly and her board chair twice a month and attended board meetings as well, providing advice on the board governance best practices. As the board became more educated about their roles and responsibilities and the transition from a founding board to a governance board took place, Holly's leadership style quickly emerged. I believe all she needed was someone to believe in her (which I did). I also worked with the board to make sure that Holly's future performance evaluation was clearly based on agreed upon goals, not personal innuendos.

The board made dramatic changes over the course of a year, some members resigned and new members were appointed. The board stopped micromanaging Holly which allowed her the opportunity to take charge and demonstrate her true leadership ability. The board chair resigned due to a new business opportunity and a delightful woman who is also a cancer survivor was appointed board chair. The new board chair took the helm and created a very positive environment for everyone to work in. Holly and the new board chair immediately developed a great personal and working relationship. Today, Holly feels more respected and supported by the board. Holly is much happier, the board understands the difference between their respective roles and responsibilities, and the staff has bought into a new vision as well.

Holly has dramatically increased her leadership potential. She knows who she is and she is a tremendous asset to her organization. Sometimes everyone just needs a friend to listen and be supportive.

RELEASING THE POWER
OF VISIONING

*"The single defining quality of leadership is
the capacity to create and realize a vision."*
William Bennis, On Becoming a Leader

An effective and strong leader "visions" the future for his or her organization. Mission answers the question, "Why do we exist?" Vision, however, answers the question, "Where do we want to go?" This is an important question because a leader sets the course for a new direction or future view of the organization. It takes courage to set the vision. Leaders of nonprofits can get caught up in the day-to-day challenges of managing the organization. Still, a leader's responsibility is to create the vision and build a strategic plan to make that vision become a reality.

This chapter will address the following ways to release the power of your organization's vision:

+ Creating the Vision
+ Operationalizing the Plan
+ Re-Examining the Mission
+ Communicating Key Achievements
+ Measuring Value and Brand Identity
+ Increasing the "Stock Price"

The old management theory was that the board set the vision and management implemented the plan to achieve it. Today, a leader must work in a true partnership with the board to create the future direction of the organization. Take the initiative in creating your organization's vision. Effective leaders develop and communicate their vision first; they do not wait for their boards to create the vision.

According to Burt Nanus, an expert in visionary leadership and the author of several books on leadership, a vision is a "realistic, credible, attractive future for your organization. It is your articulation of a destination toward which your organization should aim, a future that in important ways is better, more successful, or more desirable for your organization than is the present. Vision is a signpost pointing the way for all who need to understand what the organization is and where it intends to go." Your vision should clarify your organization's purpose and direction, set standards of excellence, inspire enthusiasm, encourage commitment, be well articulated and easily understood. Above all, your vision should be ambitious.

When I first became the president and chief executive of a medical center, the vision that I inherited from the previous administration was "to become the best community hospital in New Jersey." I asked myself, what does this mean? How was anyone going to measure the hospital's success? What criteria would be used to judge whether the organization had succeeded in reaching this vision? Though this vision might have been appropriate at a pep rally for the staff, it did not have any long-term value for the organization.

I reminded everyone that the reason that our medical center existed, the only reason they were employed, was to treat our patients and their families with courtesy and respect and to provide the highest level of quality care possible, period! I also let everyone know, in the strongest terms possible, that the patient satisfaction scores that our medical center received from patient questionnaires which ranked us at the bottom quartile of all hospitals in the country were completely unacceptable. Everyone, from senior managers to staff level employees, was told that they were responsible and accountable for our patient satisfaction scores. I established a goal for our medical center to reach the top 25% in patient satisfaction of all hospitals countrywide within the next two years. This goal became my rallying cry. The employees, medical staff and volunteers worked very hard over the next two years and we exceeded our initial goal. Our patient satisfaction scores were in the top 1% in the country for both emergency room and inpatient care and our scores for ambulatory care exceeded the top 10%. The medical center achieved a national award from a prestigious patient satisfaction survey company.

> *"You are never too old to set another*
> *goal or to dream a new dream."*
> C. S. Lewis

We followed this success with establishing a new vision for the medical center. As an outgrowth of a board retreat that I facilitated, we created a new vision: to become one of the top 100 teaching hospitals in the country. Whereas the old vision of becoming the best community hospital in New Jersey lacked a way to measure our success, our new vision had specific criteria to meet. To be considered by a national hospital benchmarking firm as a top 100 hospital, we needed to meet criteria that involved both financial and expense standards, quality improvement criteria (such as mortality and morbidity ratios) and balance sheet performance measures. Within a few years, the medical center was recognized by the organization that rated the top 100 hospitals as one of the most improved hospitals in the country.

Questions:
- What is your organization's vision for the future?
- Do you have a personal vision for your organization?
- Do you passionately believe in it today?
- Has the organization's vision become stale and in need of revitalization?

"To accomplish great things, we must not only act, but also to dream; not only plan, but also believe."
Anatole France

Creating the Vision

What is the best way to develop your organization's vision for the future and realize your organization's potential? There is no one right answer. However, there are a number of ways to accomplish this important task.

1. Develop a steering committee to create several potential options for the board to consider. One exercise is to have each member of the committee describe (in general terms) their

vision for the organization. Then, write each vision on a flip chart and ask the group the following questions of each one:

- Would our constituents (customers, patients, etc.), board members, donors, management, and staff support this vision?
- Would this vision further support our mission?
- Does this vision generate passion, excitement and commitment?
- Does this vision create a desire among the board to achieve and implement it?

2. Schedule a board planning retreat to discuss the critical issues facing the organization. List these issues in order of fundamental importance. Then, discuss with the board ways that each critical issue may be resolved or addressed. After discussing all of your critical issues and ways to address and resolve them, the future direction of your organization may become clearer.

3. Instead of focusing your attention on the critical issues at the board planning retreat (as in the last suggestions), discuss the major goals that you would like your organization to achieve. After lengthy discussion and agreement on the organization's goals, a picture of your organization will probably develop.

4. Find a comfortable chair or take a hike in a pleasant environment without any distractions and dream of your organization's future. Do

not allow your present day-to-day challenges
to limit your horizons. Dream about the ideal
situation for your organization and consider
that dream to be your organization's vision.

Creating a vision for your organization can be a highly
motivating tool for everyone to align themselves with and to
inspire everyone to produce the desired outcome: achieving
your organization's vision and realizing your organization's
potential.

> *"Intellectual strategies alone will not motivate*
> *people. Only a company with a real mission or*
> *sense of purpose that comes out of an intuitive or*
> *spiritual dimension will capture people's hearts.*
> *And you must have people's hearts to inspire*
> *the hard work required to realize a vision."*
> John Naisbitt and Patricia Aburdene,
> Reinventing the Corporation

Now that you have built a consensus on the future
direction of your organization, ask yourself these
questions:

+ How will you achieve your vision?
+ What are the right strategies necessary to
  accomplish it?
+ What specific actions will be taken? By
  whom? When?

The answers to these questions are determined by
developing an organizational strategic plan. There are
several key points to remember when developing a strategic
plan:

1. Engage as many of your key stakeholders as possible in developing your plan. People become more committed to the plan when they have had a chance to participate in its development.

2. Stay focused on the important issues and goals that you are trying to achieve. I have seen too much time and energy wasted on people spending time on issues and information that is not critical to an organization's future.

3. Keep the process as simple as possible. Don't make it any more complex than is necessary.

4. Obtain good ideas from everyone. Listen to all points of view. Allow people to speak candidly about their hopes for your organization and what they would like to see accomplished.

5. Build a plan that is connected to people's heartfelt emotions. If people are not passionate about the plan, they will not participate in its implementation at the level required for success.

6. Assign specific responsibilities, actions, and timelines for each agreed upon strategic goal. Make sure that everyone knows what is expected of them. Constantly focus on results and deal decisively with all the obstacles your organization faces in producing the desired outcome.

7. Be fluid (circumstances may change) and be prepared to modify your implementation plan based on new information, competitor analysis, new opportunities that have become

available, and other important data that you discover.

8. Communicate and market your plan to everyone and keep all stakeholders informed of the status of your implementation, recent achievements and successes.

9. Develop a list of success factors for measuring and monitoring your progress.

10. Update your strategic plan on an as-needed basis. Some organizations update their plans annually while others re-do their plans every two to three years.

There are many books on strategic planning. In the Bibliography, I have provided the names of a few books that will be helpful to you in guiding your efforts.

> *"The journey of a thousand miles*
> *begins with one step."*
> *Arthur Ashe*

Operationalizing the Plan

After developing your organization's strategic vision, the next step is to develop and implement a plan to achieve it. First, develop the key goals that have to be reached for the vision to become a reality. My suggestion is to develop somewhere between two to four goals. Organizations that have too many goals often achieve none. The best goals have the following five characteristics:

1. Specific - they must be clear and easily understood.
2. Measurable - if your goals are not measurable, you will never know if you are achieving them.
3. Attainable - they must be realistic, yet a bit of a stretch to achieve.
4. Relevant - they must be an important tool in reaching your organization's vision.
5. Timetables - they must have beginning and ending points.

The next step is to develop specific strategies and actions necessary to achieve each goal. Some goals can be worked on concurrently, while others have to follow the completion of a prior goal. Assign responsibilities for each strategy and action. Team groups are acceptable, but remember that in any business, individuals are held responsible and accountable for achieving the results that are expected of them. Monitor the progress of each goal and, if necessary, modify the strategies and actions to make sure that the desired result is achieved.

In addition to developing your vision and implementing your strategic plan to achieve your goals, it is also vitally important for today's leaders to accomplish the following:

- Re-examine the mission
- Communicate key achievements
- Measure value and brand identity
- Increase the 'Stock Price"

> *"A small body of determined spirits fired
> by an unquenchable faith in their mission
> can alter the course of history."*
> Mohandas Gandhi

Re-Examining the Mission

Have you ever participated in a board meeting for a nonprofit organization that went something like this?

"Good morning, everyone. I would like to call the meeting to order. Do I hear a motion to approve the minutes for our last meeting? Thanks, Michael. Do I have a second? Holly seconds the motion. Okay, the first item on our agenda today is to have a discussion on why we exist."

Does this sound familiar? Probably not. Being passionate about your mission is crucial if you want your organization to *unlock its true potential*. To have passion, you must have a deep understanding of why your organization exists. Understanding why your organization exists could be challenging for you, especially if your organization has been in existence for a number of years. You could be offering so many services that it is now difficult for you to easily state why you exist.

Successful organizations know that they must focus. Sometimes organizations try to take on too much. They try to do too many things and don't really excel at any of them. Leadership requires one to periodically re-examine their missions.

Questions:
+ Are you passionate about your mission?
+ Are you living up to your original mission and purpose?

+ When was the last time that you really re-examine your organization's mission or purpose?

So often we get caught up in our committee reports of finance, fundraising, strategic planning, etc., that occasionally we need to step back and examine our mission – who we are and what we're doing.

Do you remember the movie "It's a Wonderful Life" with James Stewart and Donna Reed? It is a great story about a businessman, George Bailey, who, with the help of his guardian angel, Clarence, sees what life would have been like if he did not exist. Although he was down and out and contemplating suicide in the beginning of the movie, the story has a happy ending because George realizes what a "wonderful life" he has really had.

Just as in "It's a Wonderful Life," you must do the same thing with your organization: imagine what life would be like if your women's support center, children's cancer network, family services center, or your arts and cultural organization did not exist. The answer to why you exist lies in all the wonderful things that you do that wouldn't happen without you. Know what those wonderful things are, celebrate them and be proud of them everyday.

Questions:
+ What would happen if your organization went out of business?
+ What impact would it have on your key stakeholders?
+ What impact would it have on you?

*"Spectacular achievement is always preceded
by unspectacular preparation."
Robert H. Schuller*

Communicating Key Achievements

When was the last time you examined your organization's achievements?

Spend some time thinking about the achievements that you are most proud of. What did you achieve last year? What did you achieve this year? Last month? Now that you have listed your achievements, the next step is to communicate them. Your stakeholders should know about them. Don't be modest and don't be afraid to toot your own horn. Organizations that effectively communicate their achievements and successes are often highly successful in fundraising. This is not a coincidence.

Questions:
+ Do you regularly communicate your achievements?
+ How do your staff and board know about your achievements?
+ How does the community know about your successes?
+ How do your donors and prospective donors know about your achievements?

Measuring Value and Brand Identity

What is your organization's image in the community? To *unlock your organization's true potential,"* you must establish your brand, your organization's name, as a positive image. To do this, you have to know the value you provide and establish that value in the community. Effective leaders know that establishing value through branding is for nonprofits as well as Fortune 500 companies. Please spend some time answering the following questions:

+ How do you measure your success?
+ How do you measure your value in the community?
+ What is the image of your organization in the community?
+ Has your organization performed an image tracking study?

Increasing the "Stock Price"

I often ask the executives and board members of nonprofit organizations the following question: "What's your stock price selling for today?" Of course, the immediate answer is, "We are a nonprofit 501(c) (3) corporation and don't have stock or ownership." While this is, indeed, true, the idea of a stock price is applicable to nonprofits. Effective nonprofit leaders know their "stock prices" and they want stakeholders to get a positive return on their investment in their organizations. To *unlock your organization's true potential*, you need to know what affects your stock price. The price of your stock is affected by the following:

+ Your achievements.
+ The reputation of your leaders.
+ How effective your communication strategy is.
+ Successful friend and fund development activities.
+ Board members who enjoy service on your board and proudly communicate their

membership to their friends and business associates.
+ Continuous demonstration of the purposefulness of your mission.
+ The ability to create a winning attitude among employees, board members and donors.

Questions:
+ What is your "stock price" today?
+ Has it increased or decreased over the past year?
+ What are your plans to increase it this year?

Why are some organizations able to *unlock their organization's true potential* while others are not? The answer lies in the successful organizations having a vision that is compelling and where all stakeholders are committed and passionate about achieving. Successful organizations have an unending search or quest for excellence in all they do. They constantly re-examine themselves, from top to bottom. They set expectations for their staff and board, they communicate those expectations, and they hold people accountable for measuring up. The successful organizations promote themselves extremely well. In fact, they over communicate their success. And, most importantly, they create a winning attitude and convey the message among all key stakeholders that their organization is "the place to be."

Leaders who create a vision and develop a plan to achieve its goals, while at the same time communicating their success and achievements, who develop a positive brand identity, who define the value that they provide to the community, who measure and report on their success *release the power of their visioning.*

> *"Better to light one small candle*
> *than to curse the darkness."*
> *Chinese Proverb*

Let's now turn to untapping your philanthropic success necessary to provide you with the resources to *unlock your organization's true potential.*

CASE STUDY
RELEASING THE POWER OF VISIONING

Bergen Community College

Dr. G. Jeremiah Ryan (Jerry) is a very personable chief executive, with an excellent reputation as a recognized scholar, author, and teacher. As President of Bergen Community College, one of the largest community colleges in the nation, Jerry is extremely passionate about creating educational environments where both students and faculty can excel. He is also committed to creating partnerships with public and private institutions as part of fulfilling the College's mission. "One of the College's major strategic goals is civic engagement, encouraging people to get involved in government, volunteerism, and philanthropy," said Dr. Ryan.

Dr. Ryan reached out to my firm, Dennis C. Miller Associates, Inc., to assist in developing an educational forum where citizens could learn to participate in the management and leadership of New Jersey's nonprofit community. Together with the College, I created the Nonprofit Institute for Philanthropy and Leadership. An advisory board of many of the community's top executives from the nonprofit sector was assembled to assist in developing the Nonprofit Institute.

A major symposium on nonprofit leadership was hosted by the College with over 250 chief executives, board members, development officers and volunteers attending featuring key speakers, panelists and instructors on a wide range of topics. The symposium served as a "kick off" to a Fall seminar series of courses on leadership and philanthropy. Two certificate programs were developed as a result of the seminar series: Certificate on Nonprofit Leadership and Certificate on Philanthropy, resulting in the College becoming an approved CFRE International Continuing Education Partner.

The College's Nonprofit Institute has recently developed and approved an Associate Degree in Nonprofit Management in the School of Business, Social Sciences and Public Service. "We've talked to the administration at many four year colleges about having them offer a bachelor's degree in nonprofit management, for which our courses could be used to provide credit. We are hoping that they will be ready to begin at the same time that our courses start in the Fall of 2010," Dr. Ryan recently indicated.

The College's Nonprofit Institute is perhaps one of very few community colleges in the nation to offer an Associate Degree in Nonprofit Management. The College has applied for membership in the Nonprofit Academic Centers Council, a membership association comprised of academic centers or programs at accredited colleges and universities that focus on the study of nonprofit organizations, volunteerism and/or philanthropy. Established in 1991, NACC is the first group entirely dedicated to the promotion and networking of centers that provide research and education in philanthropy and the nonprofit sector.

One of the major goals of the College's advisory board is to develop internships and cooperative educational opportunities for students and older adults seeking reemployment training in the nonprofit sector to allow them to gain "hands on" practical experiences to help them in their self-concept, decision making skills and career development. All members of the advisory board are active participants in making the Nonprofit Institute a tremendous success and are deeply committed to helping the students by serving as mentors in their professional development.

Dr. Ryan has a vision to "create community partnerships" and encourages his students to become vital and informed participants in the life of our county, state and country. Thankfully, Jerry is an expert in "releasing the power of visioning" which will benefit students and society for many years to come. I am grateful to call Jerry a friend and a client.

UNTAPPING PHILANTHROPIC SUCCESS

*"If service is the rent you pay for your existence
on this earth, are you behind in your rent."*
Robert G. Allen

Every nonprofit organization relies upon the philanthropic support of others to ensure that the necessary resources are available to carry out their mission. Hundreds of books and articles have been written on the subject of fundraising along with extensive research on the subject. Thousands of professionals attend annual conferences hosted by professional associations covering a wide range of topics on annual giving, major gifts, capital campaigns, donor software systems and online donor technologies. Yet, despite all of the knowledge about fundraising, most nonprofit organizations struggle. One of the major reasons is the inability to engage their boards. My goal in this final chapter is to teach you the process of "untapping the philanthropic success of your organization."

Questions:
+ Does your organization struggle with fundraising?
+ Would you like your board to be more fully engaged in your fundraising initiatives?

+ Would you like to increase your donors and dollars?

This chapter will address the following:
+ How to Engage Your Board
+ Development is NOT a Department
+ Principles of Philanthropy
+ Investment Theory vs. Tin Cup Theory of Fundraising
+ The Role of the Board
+ Successful Fundraising Characteristics of Nonprofits

You may be asking yourself at this point in the book, what does improving board governance, increasing leadership potential and releasing the power of visioning have to do with fundraising and philanthropy? What does it have to do with your organization? It sounds great, but what does it mean for you? *The answer is simple – it has everything to do with how well you will do convincing donors to contribute to you.*

Those organizations who successfully develop and practice excellent board governance, whose board members are deeply passionate about their mission and excited about where they are going, whose leaders are passionate, inspirational, well trusted and respected, do dramatically better in fundraising than their counterparts that do not have effective board governance, inspirational leaders and visionary thinking.

Engaging Your Board

I am often asked the following question: How can I engage and motivate my board to become truly passionate about our mission and actively participate with confidence in our fundraising initiatives. One of the major ways to increase your board's level of engagement is to *increase their level of confidence.* Far too often we have unrealistic expectations of our board members related to fundraising. Just because someone has a reputation for being a successful business or community leader, it does not translate to success in the world of philanthropy. In addition, constantly reminding someone about their fundraising role and responsibility as a board member is like reminding your kids to clean their rooms. It rarely works (perhaps your kids but not mine). When people become confident in their abilities, they generate their own motivation. I will discuss more about confidence building later in the chapter.

In addition to confidence building, the following actions are required by your leadership:

- Create a meaningful and fulfilling board experience. Tap into their unique experience and knowledge and ask them to bring new ideas to the table and ask questions. Don't allow them to leave their talents and common sense at the door.
- Encourage them to become leaders and partners in your success. The more the board member feels responsible for your success, the more he or she will become engaged.
- Develop a results oriented organization that constantly strives for excellence. When the entire organization is committed to achievement, the board will become more

committed to ensuring that you have the necessary resources.

+ Periodically re-examine your mission and purpose. Passion develops once a deeper understanding of why your organization exists is internalized. The higher the level of passion, the greater the level of engagement.

+ Discuss the outcomes and results of your programs and services, not just the activities of each. Develop measures of success and monitor your progress. The board will become more engaged in fundraising when you can demonstrate your success to the community.

+ Inquire about the image of the organization in the community and be prepared to address ways to improve it, if necessary. The board will feel more comfortable raising money when your organization has a solid reputation than one with a poor image.

+ Communicate your achievements to all stakeholders, especially your board members. By developing effective marketing and communication strategies, you can create a positive brand identity.

+ Ensure that your board can comfortably answer the following three questions:
    - What value does our organization provide to the community?
    - How do we measure our success?
    - Why are we worthy of someone's gift?

◆ Create a winning attitude among all stakeholders. Everyone likes to become associated with a winning team. Sports fans proudly wave their team's flags and colors when they are winning. Your board members will proudly "wave your flag" when you are winning too.

Development is NOT a Department

Many organizations that I know often view the development office as another department – like human resources, quality improvement or finance. Their development efforts are disconnected from the work of the organization – their boards do not see the connection between the organization's success and the success of their fundraising efforts. Often the board members have very little knowledge and experience with philanthropy and have unrealistic expectations of the staff. They wonder why development officers often move from place to place year after year.

Let me know if the following statement describes your organization – *board members would rather "stick pins" in their eyes than have anything to do with fundraising.* The mere mention of the word creates a great deal of anxiety and discomfort. Why is this? There are a number of reasons, but the biggest is the fear of rejection – if I can ask someone for money for my organization and they say no, I will feel rejected (who wants to feel rejected?). Another reason is the feeling that if I ask them for money, they will ask me for money.

Have you ever experienced the following?

Your board development committee meets —they review the fundraising plan for the upcoming year - there is talk about a gala – who can they honor this year – where should it be held? Where is the golf outing going to be? Will anyone agree to be the committee chair? How about wine tasting – how much will it cost? How much can we raise? The committee reviews the standard list of donor prospects that were assigned to each member – the committee chair asks "Did anyone call their list of prospects?" A long silence and then "OK, let's move on to discuss the table settings. Let's put it back on the agenda for next month, hopefully more people will attend the meeting." Leaving little accomplished – little achieved.

Questions:
+ Does this sound familiar?
+ How do successful organizations overcome this?
+ How do they differ from the rest?

The overwhelming number of people who serve on your boards are well meaning people, they want to do the right thing – they want your organization to succeed – but why doesn't it happen – why does everything that deals with fundraising feel like pulling teeth?

Another way to increase the board's level of engagement is to increase their knowledge of why people give money.

The Principles of Philanthropy

Board members from successful organizations understand the key principles of philanthropy – why people give money. Based on numerous experts in fundraising, the following are the key reasons why people give money:

+ They give because they want to (no arm twisting).
+ They give because they have been asked.
+ They give to people that they know and respect.
+ They give to success – not distress.
+ They give to opportunities – not needs.
+ They give to make the world a better place to be.

As previously mentioned, far too often many nonprofit executives have extremely unrealistic expectations of their board members when it comes to fundraising. During the board recruitment process, many organizations do not even bring the subject up for discussion. Yet, they expect their boards to know about fundraising and become disappointed when their performance is less than expected. We need to continually educate our board members on why people give money. The more knowledgeable and comfortable your board members become, the more their level of engagement will increase. In addition to the personal satisfaction and joy that comes from giving, one of the major reasons why people give money is because someone they know and respected asked them to. It is often as simple as that – someone asked them to give. It is very important to now discuss two other key reasons why people give – to success and to opportunities.

Investment Theory vs. Tin Cup Theory of Fundraising

Most people's concept of fundraising is the "tin cup theory of fundraising." Growing up as a young boy in New Jersey, I can always remember the poor person with one leg holding up a tin cup with pencils in front of the Port Authority bus station when I went with my mom to visit

New York City during the Christmas holidays. Many organizations still practice and promote the concept of asking for money based on their needs. Their fundraising plans and communications center on their needs for larger facilities, additional staff, operating support, new program development, etc. Your organizational needs and the resources required to obtain them are important. However, the point that I am making is to remember that rarely do people give to "needs and distress" any more, but to success and opportunities to make a difference in the lives of others. Your fundraising efforts will become more successful when you begin to frame your fundraising discussions on investing in your success.

Those organizations that have transitioned from the "tin cup theory of fundraising" to the "investment theory" have far more success in raising money. Their board members ask people to invest in their success, to produce positive results and outcomes, to continue their achievements and to make a difference in the lives of others. They no longer feel that it is personal to ask someone for money, but based on the need for investing in your success. These board members are externally focused on what they do for others and not on what the needs of the organization are. Those organizations that develop a culture where board members fully understand the principles of philanthropy and adopt the investment theory of fundraising dramatically increase their level of success in today's fierce competition for the donor dollar.

The Role of the Board

I have often been asked what the role and responsibilities of the board should be as it relates to fundraising. As part of your board orientation and ongoing educational activities, I would strongly recommend the following ten responsibilities:

+ Advocate for your mission
+ Communicate your achievements
+ Participate in special events
+ Identify and cultivate prospective donors
+ Provide input on the gift potential of others
+ Write personal notes and letters on annual appeals
+ Make an annual personal gift based on their ability
+ Ask someone for a gift (or become a co-solicitor)
+ Recognize and thank your donors

And the most important responsibility of all is to build an organization that is professional, energetic, accountable, successful and worthy of someone's gift.

Successful Fundraising Characteristics of Nonprofits

Jerold Panas is the successful author of a number of best selling books on fundraising. Two of his most popular books are "Asking: A 59 Minute Guide to Everything Board Members, Volunteers, and Staff Must Know to Secure the Gift" and "The Fundraising Habits of Supremely Successful Boards: A 1-Hour Guide to Ensuring Your Organization's Future." These books are an excellent resource guide for your board members, especially for those new to fundraising or when you are about to launch a major campaign.

I would like to mention some of the key characteristics of successful fundraising organizations according to Jerold Panas:

+ Integrity rules
+ Mission is everything
+ Never lose sight that their organization changes lives
+ Continually push for success
+ Willing to leave comfort zone
+ Extremely passionate about their organization
+ Maintain positive attitude
+ Have a strategic plan with stretch goals
+ Do not micromanage
+ Organization is one of the top philanthropic priorities of their board members
+ Constantly seek key people to join their board
+ Members attend and are prepared for board meetings
+ Board members ask people to give
+ They constantly acknowledge and thank donors

It is a great exercise during a board retreat on fundraising to ask your board members what are the successful fundraising characteristics of nonprofits. Compare their answers with the above research by Panas. When your board begins to connect integrity, passion and attitude with fundraising success, you will be on your way to *untapping your organization's philanthropic success.*

CASE STUDY
UNTAPPING PHILANTHROPIC SUCCESS

CPC Behavioral Healthcare

John Mans, CPA, is the President & CEO of CPC Behavioral Healthcare (CPC), the largest provider of behavioral healthcare services in Monmouth County, New Jersey. John is an outstanding leader with a strong commitment to helping others in need, and his financial and managerial expertise is a valuable asset in ensuring that CPC's mission to promote wellness, recovery and productive lives is maintained. CPC's vision is to be the provider of choice for individuals and families dealing with behavioral, emotional or substance abuse disorders, developmental disabilities and special education needs in the regional community they serve.

CPC had recently completed a three year strategic plan for his organization. In order to have the necessary financial resources to implement the plan, John contacted Dennis C. Miller Associates, Inc., and asked our help in developing a strategic fundraising plan to support the goals of the strategic plan. In addition, John wanted help in engaging his boards to more fully participate in the fundraising initiatives of CPC. In order to develop such a plan, we first reviewed a detailed list of information from the client, including the newly developed strategic plan, board structures and committees, board minutes, and current fundraising operations. Interviews were conducted with all 20 members of his board, executive team and chief development officer.

Interviewees were asked a series of open ended questions about the organization to ascertain their level of passion and engagement with CPC, their understanding of the vision and mission, their roles and responsibilities as it related to fundraising, their achievements and how those achievements were communicated to all key stakeholders, and their image in the community. Organizations that have strong board governance, a compelling strategic vision, positive image in the community and keen understanding of philanthropy do extremely well with fundraising results.

We helped the organization develop a comprehensive strategic fundraising plan and made a series of specific recommendations to: improve the board structure, committees and board skills; enhance marketing and communications/branding strategies; and strengthen board giving, leadership gifts, corporate and foundation grants and their special events. Our plan also included a Case for Support with the organization's mission and vision, record of achievements, the difference in the lives of those served, what they were raising money for, ways to give and why the donor would benefit from giving a gift.

Since our report was issued, the organization has seen a dramatic increase in both board and individual gifts, greater brand/awareness presence in the community, a more engaged board with a clear understanding of their roles and responsibilities, and a new willingness of key leaders to join their board.

John's persistence and determination to fully engage his board was difficult to accomplish early on. Changing cultures is very difficult to do, especially in a short period of time. There were many board members who had been on various boards of the organization for many years. But through the development of the board's leadership, success became a reality. The more the board became fully aware of all of the accomplishments of the organization, the more they became willing to participate in "giving and getting" personal donations. Prior to that, CPC had relied almost exclusively on special event fundraising.

As CPC is about to celebrate its 50th anniversary, the level of board giving has dramatically increased to record levels. John has certainly learned the process of *untapping his philanthropic success*. I am glad to consider John a good friend and a client.

BRINGING IT ALL TOGETHER

I hope that *The Nonprofit Board Therapist: A Guide to Unlocking Your Organization's True Potential* has provided you with the inspiration and motivation to develop the confidence and courage to pursue your organization's dreams and goals. I also hope that you feel a greater sense of purpose that empowers and enables you to increase your leadership potential, to feel better about what you can do, thereby allowing you to approach your work with passion, high energy and a positive attitude.

I strongly believe that every organization has the ability to *unlock its true potential*. I have seen numerous organizations develop their potential by constantly improving who they are, what they do, and how they communicate their success and achievements. These successful organizations all exhibit a deep commitment to excellence in all facets of their organizational life. They integrate board governance, leadership, visionary thinking and philanthropy. They have the courage and strength to constantly re-examine their board and leadership performance to make any necessary improvements, despite how uncomfortable these changes may feel at first. They are led by confident and competent chief executives and board leaders who inspire everyone to seek new ways to achieve their goals.

It takes a tremendous amount of hard work to *unlock their true potential*, it does not happen overnight. One of the keys to their success is their determination and commitment to overcome the many obstacles that have to be dealt with. Whether your organization's obstacles are poor board governance, ineffective leadership, a stale vision that no longer motivates or inspires your stakeholders, a poor image in the community and/or a lackluster fundraising strategy, you can overcome this by following the steps outlined in the book.

One of the main reasons why so many organizations *do not unlock their true potential* is their inability to be honest with themselves in their assessments. They know they have problems, e.g., ineffective board or executive leadership, but they fail to address it. They hope that the problems will just go away. Problems don't go away; they just get repressed and destroy the will of the organization. Leadership is required for success. I have seen far too many organizations with tremendous potential that never develops because the board does not want to provide the chief executive with honest and constructive criticism. The executive is told about what they do well, but there is a tendency to avoid any discussion about negative performance issues such as not getting along with people, how people may perceive them and/or their ineffectiveness in getting results. People grow and develop through self awareness. It is extremely important to provide individuals with feedback on how they are doing and what they need to improve upon. By avoiding the issue, the organization suffers and little is achieved.

The same is true for ineffective board leadership. The board, not the chief executive, must step up to the plate and develop a plan to address the performance issue in a non-confrontational manner. No one enjoys having to deal with confrontation, especially with regard to a professional colleague. To *unlock your organization's true potential*, every board member needs to work together towards achieving the goals of the organization, bringing fulfillment and meaning to all who serve on the board.

Leaders who create a compelling and inspirational vision and develop a plan to achieve its goals, while at the same time communicating their successes and achievements, which develop a positive brand identity, which define and articulate the value their organization provides to the community, who measure and report on their success, *unlock their organization's true potential.* Successful organizations have an unending search or quest for excellence in all they do. They constantly re-examine themselves, from top to bottom. They set expectations for their chief executive, board and staff, they communicate those expectations, and they hold people accountable for measuring up. They over-communicate their success and convey the message among all key stakeholders that their organization is "the place to be."

Every nonprofit relies upon the philanthropic support of others to ensure that the necessary resources are available to carry out their mission. The difficulty that many organizations have is the inability to fully engage their boards in fundraising. By transitioning from the "tin cup theory" to the "investment theory," board members are more likely to increase their level of engagement in fundraising. Board members can relate better to the concept of investments. They are more confident and knowledgeable about participating in the cultivation and solicitation of prospective donors.

Organizations that are successful put a face on their organization – they appeal to both your heart and your mind. They explain who they are, where they are going and how they make a difference in the lives of others. They communicate their success and ask you to invest in their success – they demonstrate how the donor benefits in this relationship, not just in how their organization benefits.

By integrating and improving all key components of an effective organization – board governance, leadership development, visionary thinking and philanthropy - your organization will *unlock its true potential* and continue to make the lives of people better for today and tomorrow.

BIBLIOGRAPHY

Adubato, Steve, and Theresa Foy DiGeronimo. *Speak from the Heart: Be Yourself and Get Results.* Free Press. 2002.

Barry, Bryan W. *Strategic Planning Workbook for Nonprofit Organizations, revised and updated.* Amherst H. Wilder Foundation. 1997

Bobowick, Marla J., Sandra R. Hughes and Berit M. Lakey. *Transforming Board Structure, Strategies for Committees and Task Forces.* BoardSource, 2003.

Chait, Richard P., William P. Ryan, and Barbara E. Taylor. *Governance as Leadership: Reframing the Work of the Nonprofit Board.* John Wiley & Sons, 2004

Harvard Business School Press (editor). *Becoming an Effective Leader (The Results Driven Manager Series).* Harvard Business School Press. 2005.

Howe, Fisher. *The Nonprofit Leadership Team.* San Francisco, Jossey-Bass, 2004

Kocsis, Deborah L., and Susan A. Waechter. *Driving Strategic Planning: A Nonprofit Executive's Guide.* BoardSource, 2003.

Light, Mark. *The Strategic Board: The Step- by- Step Guide to Higher-Impact Governance.* John Wiley & Sons, 2001.

Lakey, Berit M; Sandra R. Hughes and Outi Flynn. *Governance Committee. BoardSource Committee Series.* BoardSource, 2004.

Miller, Dennis C., *A Guide to Achieving New Heights: The Four Pillars of Successful Nonprofit Leadership.* AuthorHouse. 2007.

Panas, Jerold. *The Fundraising Habits of Supremely Successful Nonprofit Boards.* Emerson & Church Publishers.

Rosso, Hank. *Achieving Excellence in Fundraising.* San Francisco: Jossey- Bass, 2003.

ABOUT THE AUTHOR

Dennis C. Miller is the President and CEO of Dennis C. Miller Associates, Inc., a Denville, New Jersey firm that specializes in board governance, leadership development and strategic planning services to the nonprofit community. Dennis has 30 years of experience working as both a consultant and executive with numerous nonprofit organizations, including healthcare, human services, public benefit and educational institutions.

In addition to his firm, Dennis is the Director of the Nonprofit Institute for Leadership at Bergen Community College in Paramus, New Jersey, one of the largest community colleges in the nation. Dennis, in conjunction with college officials, developed both certificate and academic degree programs in Leadership.

Dennis was also President and CEO of Somerset Medical Center, a major New Jersey teaching medical center and healthcare foundation, from 1999 to 2004. Under the leadership of Dennis, the medical center became one of the premier medical centers in New Jersey. He is also a Fellow of the American College of Health Care Executives. Dennis is an experienced board chair, has served on many nonprofit boards and chaired numerous board committees.

Dennis has an undergraduate degree from Rutgers University in Social Sciences and a Master's Degree in Health Administration and Policy from Columbia University's Mailman School of Public Health.

Dennis is recognized as a national expert in all matters related to nonprofit organizations. He is a motivational speaker and frequently serves as facilitator for board retreats. Dennis brings a sense of humor, passion and wealth of personal experience and practice knowledge to his clients. Dennis is the author of his first book, "A Guide to Achieving New Heights: The Four Pillars of Successful Nonprofit Leadership" and a former columnist on board governance for The NonProfit Times.

Please visit www.dcmillerassociates.com for more information about Dennis C. Miller Associates, Inc.

Dennis can be reached at dennis@dcmillerassociates.com.